IN SUN'S SHADOW

Praise for *In Sun's Shadow*

Personal, philosophical, social, nature-oriented—all of these adjectives characterize this book composed by a mature cosmopolitan poet. The book's opening poem ("The Fences I've Climbed Over") kicks everything off by describing the poet's struggles in life in terms of this metaphor, based on his actual escape from Hungary, his homeland, after its unsuccessful uprising against the brutal Soviet rule. Overcoming that particular obstacle, both literally and figuratively, set Paul Sohar on a journey into his new life that has taken numerous twists and turns along the way. In this book, the poet is a careful observer: "Behind the moist glasses his eyes were hard / bolts shaken out of the complex structure of a city sky," a dreamer: "Dusk clings to the windows, its charcoal / belly rubs the glint off the glass and the long / tentacles smudge up the sky, // ...Why must we know what is yet to come?" and, in the end, a father: "Life is a learning process, as we say, / we keep accumulating loaves of wisdom / for old age, / and I'm in it now but without a crumb / for my mind to nibble on / with you gone without a reason, / and I am still foolish enough to keep on asking why / on my first Father's Day alone; / an abandoned natural wonder, / overgrown with memories."

As Sohar indicates in his introductory remarks, except for the last section of the book these poems are not necessarily in chronological order, even though they represent a major portion of the poet's adult life. Indeed, *In Sun's Shadow* resonates a lifetime of experiences. It is a poignant book deftly written and overflowing with remarkable perception and imagination that highlights one of the significant poetic voices of our generation.

—Alan Britt, author of *Violin Smoke*
Towson University

IN SUN'S SHADOW

SELECTED POEMS BY Paul Sohar

RAGGED SKY PRESS
PRINCETON, NEW JERSEY

Published by Ragged Sky Press
270 Griggs Drive
Princeton, NJ 08540
http://www.raggedsky.com/

Text and cover design by Jean Foos
Front cover art is a detail from *Pretextual Reality* (1971), a painting by the
Dutch-American artist Jan ten Broeke (1930-2019) whose surrealist-abstract
art was widely exhibited in the US and Europe. He and the poet were long-
time friends; they both held a daytime job in the research labs of Merck
drug company.

ISBN : 978-1-933974-36-1
Library of Congress Control Number: 2019956518
This book has been composed in FF Scala and DIN

Printed on acid-free paper. ∞

Printed in the United States of America

Contents

Preface | ix

War & Peace

The Fences I've Climbed Over | 3 War in Snow | 4
War Bread | 5
In No Man's Land | 6
Redemption Circa 20th Century C.E. | 7
Saturday Morning in Warren | 8
Years Stalking | 9
Last Look at JFK Below | 10
Street Ballad | 11
Song of a Green-Glazed Tile | 12
The 1st Day of a Long Winter | 13
Snow-Sun of a Nor'easter | 14
Rue du Revenant | 15
Hubcap Let Loose | 16
Passing the Seventy-Mile Mark | 17
Desert Stone | 18
Up and/or Down | 19
Committing Poetry in Public | 20
Erecting New Ruins Every Day | 21
War & Peace in Budapest | 22

The Orphan Key

Rumors of the Night | 25
A Night Outside My Head | 26
Redwood Chair at Rest | 27
Chase of the Night | 28
Night Walk | 29
Echoes of a Golden Age | 30
Ex Libris | 31
The Fourth Position | 32
The Silent Dreamer | 33
The Midnight Trolley | 34
Geometric Mythology | 35

County Road | 36

Twists and Turns of Map Noir | 37

Brief Belief | 38

The City on the Hill | 39

The History of Nothing | 40

Anyway, the Doves | 41

Frying Pan Morning | 42

The Orphan Key | 43

Insomniac Dreams

The Fat Lady Sings | 47

Friday in MOMA with George | 48

Art-Drunk Midnight | 49

Short Course on Freedom | 50

Macedonian Dreams | 51

The Trees of Eden | 52

Midden of Dreams: Barefoot Flowers | 53

Dark Windows in the Fog | 54

Sunset Dives into Lake Balaton | 55

The Second Coming of Antichrist | 56

The Eighth Dwarf | 57

Monosyllabic Words | 58

Costume Drama in the Nude | 59

Rat Factory | 60

Belgian Still Life Without Canvas | 61

The Grand Bazaar | 62

Tightrope Too | 63

An Idol Not Cruel | 64

Wozzeck Paraphrases | 65

Violent Concerto No. 1 | 66

Chamber Opera in Ten Acts | 67

Insomniac Dreams | 68

The Country of the Soul

The Last Wind and the Last Man on Earth | 71

The War's Unfinished Nocturne | 72

Armistice Day Parade | 73

Free Ride | 74

Postcard from Budapest | 75

Tales from the Trap | 76

Feelings | 77

What Finality Feels Like | 78

Inside, Outside in the Jungle | 79

The Ratgod | 80

The City Wind | 81

Pedestal City Revisited | 82

Dona Mihi Pacem | 83

The Taste of Blood | 84

The Sweet Stink of Money | 85

On Exhibit | 86

Two-Sided Mistake | 87

Bombs in Armchairs | 88

Silence versus Noise | 89

The Country of the Soul | 90

From a Hiker's Diary

Hiking the Canada Dry Trail | 93

Trail to Timelessness | 94

Springing | 95

Morning Metamorphosis | 96

Stealing Mountains | 97

Mount Minsi | 98

Squirrel Gods | 99

A Night at the Opera | 100

Immortality Denied | 101

Brooklyn Bat | 102

Trans Gypsy Moth | 103

Canyon Dreams | 104

Birds of Different Feather | 105

Summer Evening Sonata | 106

Drunken Deer Eyes | 107

Discovery of the Sky | 108

Summer's Throat | 109

Sudden and Reckless Peace | 110

From A Hiker's Diary | 111

Wild Vase Poetry

The Implanted Epitaph | 115
Armageddon Again | 116
Laconic Bulls | 117
The Hero of My Childhood | 118
The Show: Sex in the Ice Age | 119
Still Life in a Shattered Mirror | 120
In Sun's Shadow | 121
Winter Dead | 122
Poetry Paraphrase | 123
A Variation on a Theme by Verlaine | 124
Two-Minute Salvation | 125
The Wild Vase | 126

The Endless End

Earth to Earth | 129
Eyes Closed | 130
Danse Macabre | 131
My Crutch | 132
The Lonely Fable | 133
The Last Xmas Tree | 134
Her Glasses | 135
The Endless End | 136
Hope | 137
Father's Day Parade | 138
Funny... | 139
Maledizione! | 140
The Weekend | 141
On an Endless Road | 142
The Lost Raindrop | 143

Acknowledgments | 144
About the Author | 147

Preface

Readers who wander into the labyrinth of these poetic lines are likely to be adventurous explorers of literature and need no Virgil to guide them; the author merely wishes to unveil the ingredients behind the titles of the seven sections that—much like chapbooks standing on their own—make up this modest volume: War & Peace—autobiographical poems; The Orphan Key—riffs on the sensations of being; Insomniac Dreams—poems on art and literature; The Country of the Soul—poems of social significance; From a Hiker's Diary—nature poems; Wild Vase Poetry—experiments in formal poetry; The Endless End—in memoriam, Camilla, mourning the recently departed daughter.

Except for the last section the poems are not arranged in chronological order, some are decades old and some quite recent. The selection process concentrated on poems that had already been published in a periodical thereby proven to make some sense and represent some aesthetic value to an outsider. Apologies to publications whose hospitality is not manifest here, but the book had to be reduced to a manageable size. Also omitted are poems already in one of the author's two books of poetry: *Homing Poems* (Iniquity Press, 2005) and *The Wayward Orchard* (Wordrunner Press, 2012). Still, some sections and even poems may overlap like the foliage of the trees in a forest, but hopefully the canopy they make will speak to the hiker.

Happy trails!

War & Peace

The Fences I've Climbed Over

the fences I've climbed over whether spiky
and high or merely made of hymns and fears
now lie harmless on the ground

but some are still standing in my way
daring me to dare them and why not?
why not I say and start climbing again

I still glance up and down and around me
to see if anyone's looking though who cares?
let them catch me and shoot me with their eyes

besides even if they're looking they don't see me
they look right through me I'm a patch of fog
and by the time they'd stare me to death

I'm already climbing over another fence
into another secret garden or forbidden pond
thick with swampy water lilies drunk on naked sunshine

and no one from the shore can tell what's growing
and what's dying in pretense who's who in the secret chase
whether I am in or out or which side of the fence

the guardians of the fence only watch one another
they think the fence is enough to stop me
but the one they stop is someone else

the fences I've climbed over are now stacked in storage
along with the fences that stopped me once, but some nights
I still borrow one to play with, hoping the night never ends

War in Snow

...and snow, too, was whiter and
more plentiful in the old days,
the whole world was disguised
in bleached hospital gowns
to make the terrain seem arctic
and confusing from above,
from the huge planes looking
for the house where I lived
to drop a deliriously explosive
xmas present
but why did it take so many planes,
so many bombs to look for me?
but let's not forget the snow
of the good old days when snow was snow,
and it came down in huge flakes,
bigger than big butterflies hurrying home,
and happy to lie down together
like us in the basement, yes,
but let's not forget the snow,
the chronic snow cover
vintage 1944–45,
all that snow and yet we didn't get
to see the butterflies coming down
that winter because the windows
in the basement were too small
and blocked with heavy beams
from the ruins next door and
the only time we went out was
between battles and to collect snow
that we melted for water on fire fueled by
broken rafters, beams and studs
from the ruins next door
there was no shortage of ruins
free for the taking

War Bread

by the end of the war we'd eat
    bread left over by the crows
bread brought back from the war
    in caskets or black envelopes
bread growing on the empty shelf
    in piles of dead maggots
by the end of the war we'd devour
    bread made of barren soil
bread whose soil was
    mocked by clay
bread kneaded by bare feet on
    the muddy road to death
bread ivan denisovich saved under his shirt
    even if he didn't have a shirt
bread dumped by the fat backsides
    of bread merchants and prison guards
and after this war we'll make our bread
    out of naked skulls and eat
the crumbs the dead will drop
    from their busy jaws
and we'll rip open one another's bellies
    for the bread
after this war there will be another war
    eating the soil without baking it into
bread and the soil will be lapping up
    toxic crumbs scattered by loaves of
war-bred clouds from an oven we
    used to call the sky

In No Man's Land

what happens to those afraid to move
frozen forever like a shadow
behind an indifferent oak

a dream can still freeze me in the drama
of my run across the border
a tableau pregnant with bullets and finales

what happens to the footsteps
frozen to the spot
not knowing which way to run

what happens to the corpses of
those shot at the border
trying to escape their scripted fate

what happens to the prayers
that turn into stones and attack
their own tired feet

what happens to the oaks
that failed to report the escapee
hiding behind them

and how do the oaks feel now
the ones that refused to tell
the hunted which way to flee

oaks are indifferent border guards
they guard neither the border
nor the shadow hiding behind them

don't look back at the border you've
crossed alive
it might come after you

Redemption Circa 20th Century C.E.

A bucket and a scrub brush once cured me of
a panic attack that ferociously clung to my throat;

those modest tools were handed to me by a priest
in a crow-black cassock with a bony smile;

we were standing in the communal restroom,
the second focal point of the refugee camp,

the first being the window where
the bowls of soup were handed out,

but before you could work in the kitchen you
had to put in some time in the restrooms,

that was the rule in the refugee camp,
and as soon as I started working with

the bucket of water and the scrub brush
I heard angels explaining to me the scheme;

the smell of the latrine smelled sweet
after smelling eternal fear for an eternal night,

after smelling the cynical stench of hell
I was overcome by a smell of revelation,

the promise of salvation handed to me with
a bucket of water and a scrub brush.

Saturday Morning in Warren

On a 30-minute walk from home into town
and back I counted 3 dead:

one raccoon, hit on the main road, bleeding to death,

one shrew flattened on my dead-end road and buzzing with flies,

one forest rat lying on its back with four legs sticking up, but
otherwise untouched, probably electrocuted on the power line.

Three dead encountered in a brisk 30-minute walk.

And I'm still around to meditate over it. But how can I,
with that brutal buzz chewing through the valley?

I wish a dragon would rise from the garbage dump
            and run over that fanatic
who's hunting fall leaves with a garrulous leaf blower
and killing the whisper of the wind in the woods.

Years Stalking

Years not content with depositing moss
on the convulsions of my concrete stoop
have been stalking me in and out
trampling all over my face
giving me grim smiles & malodorous glances
and stealing my belongings
my favorite shirts and verse-dependent diaries

I take my pills and drain my sclerotic guts
before going to bed.
I even try to close my eyes at night and
see myself as my dreams used to but it's no use
I'm kept awake all night by the stealthy steps
of years stalking my portrait done in oil long
before the years turned against me

the painting shows me holding a glass and
a cigarette or both in one hand

the wine is still the same and the glass
sits in my hand like a tyrant on a throne
but it looks past me and talks to the years around me
all waiting for me to make up my mind

but it's just a game
they've got my mind in their grubby hands
and they laugh when I say I don't care
take all you want but don't leave
this dirt curtain on my tongue
this shuffle of poisonous feet on my night

Last Look at JFK Below

what if too lukewarm
what if concrete
what if nowhere
yet in plain sight
and I forget which fork of the road
what if

not there but
you know what I mean

what if the pilot is blind
as blind as god and can't see earth
what's happening here
and what is not
what is after eight
blue with a mean streak
and not there but here
not then but now

what if you can hear me
what if deaf is a noun
what if I exist
after eight blue
what if there's no eight
no clocks
what if the unknown is
screwing with me

Street Ballad

swept into a street crowded with umbrellas
crawling over one another I protest

if I really have to walk down this cold-cursed
obstacle course I'd rather do it alone

I don't want to share my umbrella with someone
who might get wet and fault me for it

there's a trickle down my neck to my socks
the map is a soggy mess in my pocket

the last thing I need is someone to tell me
I'm headed in the wrong direction

it's easier to curse out god than someone
who needs the shelter of your umbrella

I have enough trouble trying to decode
the tap-tap of the rain knocking above me

Song of a Green-Glazed Tile

She crawls out of the potter's hands
and into the fireplace, squats
to hug the flames and kiss the glow,
it's all right I say when she claims
to be my soul.

I do feel warm drops of clay boil
out of my goose bumps; she likes
to borrow them when crawling
into the fireplace

to hug the flames with her forest
green skin and to be hugged
by the red bricks, strong rows of them
bristled with soot, by traces
of a dark but overheated night.

The 1st Day of a Long Winter

Impossible to forget!
It's all over, no point talking about it.
Don't try to confuse me.

Would you believe it?
Sure, the story has two legs,
it can go either way.

Happy holidays!
And sad holy years, covered
with prickly holy seconds.

What's your name?
I'm not from around here.
They call me the same.

I'm not from around here.
What's the problem?
Happy Holy Wars.

Tallest building, tallest lie.
Only time can tell.
And the speed of the building.

The tallest must lie down.
In the sea, to make way for
the gray wind of fear.

I'm trying to forget.
It's a great vacation spot.
Out of sight, out of mind.

What are you talking about?
Yes, I too can feel it,
It's on the tip of my tongue.

Snow-Sun of a Nor'easter

in the morning the snow-sun hangs an old
soap-splattered shower curtain over the sky and a bare
15-watt light bulb behind it, but by the afternoon

the bulb dissolves and the curtain disintegrates,
crumbling into small, weightless frazzles, dead moths,
first just a dusting and then a stampede,

and soon heaven is down here with us,
we walk on top of clouds without halos or white robes,
and our wings feel clumsy on our feet,

we alternate between feeling as light as a snowflake
and as heavy as a shovelful of snow,
we're still learning the ways of this upside-down world,

overnight the house too floats away and lands in a color-free,
enchanted forest, nothing but plain white, where silence
speaks louder than earthly traffic noise,

the day has its borders torn down, the walls of hours collapse,
minutes float off suspended on snowflakes
instead of crumbling time into hurry-up grains of sand,

our feet are still earthbound, but our eyes quickly learn to float,
and we start learning to hold our breath, to breathe in heaven
and keep it inside even after the clouds vanish under our boots

Rue du Revenant

I had to go back to the old town for my wallet I
had left behind in a café; the others stayed at
the railroad station ready to catch the train
with or without me;

there was a good chance I could make it back
in time if I hurried, the streets were all familiar
already, at every corner I knew exactly
which way to turn,

the narrow streets hugged me like a long-lost cousin,
the cobblestones cheered me on, the clock tower waved
hello, but in the meantime the café had been moved
further down Rue du Revenant, I could tell
by the umbrellas on the sidewalk;

worse yet, without the others I suddenly felt naked,
my mind stripped of sunglasses and now easily bruised
by every flapping store sign, every bicycle passing by;
I felt indecent walking through town alone,

and no wonder I could not keep up with the café
even though I broke into a trot, my naked eyeballs
bouncing up and down, but when I chased the café
outside of town, out to farm fields, I slowed down;

the café was gone and probably so was the train,
there was no point in running anymore, and there
were haystacks standing still not too far away.

Hubcap Let Loose

having tossed my id card on the boss's desk
I walked out the gate
as happy as a hubcap
a loose hubcap set free
allowed to roll down a highway
headed for the grassy strip on the shoulder
best down an open slope
rolling toward a grove of rhododendrons
that have never been cut or trimmed
to make room for more roads and trucks

I didn't feel like stopping
not even at home
I just wanted to keep rolling
afraid that once stopped
I may not know which way to go

and may even beg to be screwed
back to another wheel
maybe that of a garbage truck

Passing the Seventy-Mile Mark

the car wheels are squealing,
too many sneaky curves,
too many blinding headlights and
signs that still come as a surprise,

yet the landscape can fake
the familiar, the way its hips
befriend the sun and
the lookout points slide under the car;

perhaps the trip is already over,
and I keep going around in circles,
the hereafter comes to me
only as a valley filled with fog.

But then why the tire squeals,
why this jumper cable around my neck?
Why this empty paper cup if it's
too heavy even when I'm sitting down?

A youthful voice from other trips might call
out to me through the fog now and then.
I'm looking hard at a map that stays blank,
devoid of place names, rivers, roads,

but suddenly I hear a voice from behind
the blank stare, a voice so full of
distant vistas and beautiful sunshine:
Why don't you just come back to bed?

Desert Stone

One day I'll be a desert stone,
an odd-shaped rock, far off the road,
far from the malls of make-believe; yet
I'll be real and as sharp as any traffic sign.

I'll be standing in the desert, halfway
up an average hill; there'll be
a view below me and, just out
of my sight, a mountaintop,

a mystery I will not dream about
any more than about rolling down the hill.
I'll just stand there naked as any other rock,
my skin scraping the desert wind.

Up and/or Down

You told me
it was a long
narrow ladder
I had to climb
but you forgot
to tell me that
with every step
the last rung
would let go
and fall down
out of sight
and I forgot
to ask you
where the long
ladder would
lead. And now
I refuse to take
another step
until you tell me
or else put
all the rungs back
under me.

Committing Poetry in Public

The gum trees cried themselves silly-sticky,
he said when arrested, and the car grill frowned,
he could feel the dashboard jerk....
Yes, he was sitting there, no denying the facts,
he was caught with his pen in hand,
but the squeals all came from the car radio.

On subsequent questioning he admitted
it was a poem he was penning
but didn't finish it and probably would not have
even if he had not been caught....

Was it the big heap of black garbage bags
growing by the curb or the erect parking sign
shoved into the ashen skin of the sidewalk?
What turned him on to poetry?

The car was legally parked,
license and registration were in order,
but appearances can be deceiving.

Behind the moist glasses his eyes were hard
bolts shaken out of the complex structure of a city sky.
Only the gum trees cried,
their sticky knees offering no defense.

Erecting New Ruins Every Day

There's one under the rubble
someone still dreaming of
being found and left there
as not worthy of rescue

I'm climbing in the ruins
up on the crest of a wall
still standing
on dead bricks and dying mortar

There's life among the ruins
rats don't chew empty walls
the wind does not talk to broken windows
unless an eye is stuck behind

Come and get me and forget me
if you will but please do something
with the ruins crawling
all over the remnants of my life

There's someone climbing on
the crest of a crumbling wall
exhorting the wounded bricks
and the pus-infested mortar

to build the ruins of another life
in another city of another god who
may hold an empty holy grail for
the blood the buried souls ejaculate

War & Peace in Budapest

whether screaming or slyly silent
the streets all drown in soul-infested plazas

ghosts doodle windows on the plain walls
of the will to see the sidewalk

we don't have to look far to lick the past
with our sticky dreams and to herd the future
to the boulevards of being

I resided here long before I was born
and keep returning to bathe
in the gaze of granite ramparts

even when ripping open the neighbor's curtains
it is I who surrenders

to reside here is a sin absolved by every statue
in every park
because to breathe is the goal of every eye

even the dust is nourishing
the rain as warm as a dry blanket

in spite of its own crooked streets
life here is forever
not a momentary flash due to a glitch

dust here doesn't cover the dust of history
or the windows of tomorrow but feeds them

go shovel more dust with your feet

The Orphan Key

Rumors of the Night

dark rumors of the night
come tumbling from
the slumber-heavy foliage
but crumble into mumbles

when they roll across
the already naked road
a strip of asphalt already
asleep around the bend

the drooping foreheads
of the road signs
seem to know something's
about to happen

a day is going to sink
into the soft bed of the woods
dressed in the black silk
of intimate sheer dew

the car is already a time
machine whisking us
toward the scary headlights
of tomorrow

A Night Outside My Head

like a dog left outside with the door shut in its face
I get locked out of my head on sleepless nights
put out into the dark that cannot settle down
cannot congeal into nothingness
but keeps churning with silent forceless winds
among walking bushes
and vicious hounds trapped by their legs
but ready to trap the sleepless in their jaws

the night outside my skull is sculpted by
teeth that keep me out there in the sleepless night
I keep banging on my head
my forehead
my ears and temples
with my rusty but sharp arthritic fists
demanding to be let in
and allowed back in bed
covered by a multicolored dream blanket

but it's no use
perhaps there's no one inside my head
except emptiness from wall to wall
packed so tight that there's no room for me
not until it dries up like a receding flood
by the morning
when I am able to open the door and get back in

but by then the place looks different
the scene of an all-night party with sticky
pizza boxes and beer cans on the floor
with unmated shoes and dirty underwear mixed in
my head doesn't feel like home
after outside in a sleepless night
but I have nowhere else to go
so I might as well try and clean up the place

Redwood Chair at Rest

the redwood chair overturned
under the forsythia and overgrown
by pumpkin-colored treeless leaves
could be a dead deer
lying on its flank
with legs sticking up
defiantly in rigor mortis
unable to rest
unwilling to stop
unlike the picnic table
and the benches
laid back on their sides
holding gray silence
solemn nothingness
the ruins of summers past
the litter of fun at flirt
that died off with the chatter
of green restlessness

Chase of the Night

before the night picks up its toys
and escapes under the bed
morning sneaks in with
feline flashes of light
meowing up the windowpanes

dreams are not wanted here
morning has no use for
dream-drunk moaning

it's time to put on the light-resistant
robe of invisibility
the footwear of purpose

the light
the imperious light
too has its litter box

and it sheds its hair and skin
over the scant toys of the night
when I still feel like playing

it's easier to clean up the mess of
a defecating garbage bag
then to wash sunlight off your dreams
once it begins to purr

Night Walk

With its sinuous dance
gaslight vaporizes the cast-iron lampposts
into the cold hard darkness
of the silent street

Conversation with the pavement
stumbles to its knees,
dragging its feet behind
a penitent seeking footprints to follow

The bare bones of trees grope
the outlines of rain
then saunter toward morning
though without making a move

there's nothing more to say

The emptiness of the sidewalk
slithers around the corner
to disappear under mute
shouts of graffiti

Loneliness never loses
its longing legs or the sight of lights
even if it means getting sucked into
a street without a sign

Echoes of a Golden Age

A panoramic picture suddenly parts the forest
and steps out in front of the car, crowned with
a cloud, the kind a voice likes to hide behind.

We can almost hear it, maybe the echoes of
a golden age, except it's in an ancient tongue or
else plain gibberish, at least to us on the ground.

After snapping a few pictures we get back into
the car and follow the reluctant road down to
the flatlands below. No sky, no voice in the car

to follow us, only the promise of a picture
hidden in the microchip of the camera.
Maybe we'll understand what it has to say.

Ex Libris

Wisdom loses its velvety x-rated smile
when the chair catches on fire and
the book flaps, its covers flying off,
leaving but the dust jacket for
the reader as a hiding place.
Without the book, wisdom
has no further reason to burn
in the reader's empty hands.

The Fourth Position

The lights were out already and
the big black fluffy chest of sleep
was starting to caress them when
her voice rubbed open a tiny hole
in the silence: You know
it's the fourth position I like best,

     when the bed turns into a lost continent
     and we sail it on a myth that cannot end,
     because the god that holds me in his lap
     appears inside you and makes you grow
     into a giant who can trap not only me
     but him as well, in one marble-white legend,
     a lost continent whose skies are never spent,
     never sent to rest beside the horizon,
     never smothered by the furry chest
     of sleep or powdered into sand
     by awakenings—

it's the fourth position I like best...
her voice swims slowly back to land,
sent by the warm waves of silence, back
to the shores of her lost continent.

The Silent Dreamer

Dusk clings to the windows, its charcoal
belly rubs the glint off the glass and the long
tentacles smudge up the sky, planting
darkness in every corner of the house

in piles of shapeless grayish eggs that will
hatch during the night with cracks and squeaks
converging in a long rumble of her dream
in the shape of an eyeless snake smiling at
the dreamer's silly fright.

Why must we know what is yet to come?
Now it's the dusk to deal with, to
draw the curtains, turn on the lights
praying the titles of TV shows
and names of people to call

while the darkness builds its nest
minute by minute within the walls;
soon it'll be too late to tell her
fright is but another dream, she'll be
spinning spiderwebs of her own.

The Midnight Trolley

A gaggle of young cadavers with
ghoulish shrieks piercing their lips
take over the midnight trolley

one of them gets hold of the controls
and drives the car backwards
to the mordant cheers of unveiled teeth

a danse macabre of steel with bone
wheels cutting open the skin
of the boulevard

bull's-blood lipstick painted
on lipless jaws and pelvis bones
panting for blood

rigor mortis penetrates the eyes
as the dull gleam of the grim reaper's scythe
perforates noses and brows

death is the stillborn password
passed around in an empty urn
to be tasted by dead-groggy grins

the trolley plows through a live cemetery
on the prowl for more cadavers
to be resurrected from the living

Geometric Mythology

Rectangular is the god
of those who hate one another;
his blunt weight first flattens them,
and then his sharp corners crumple them
into schizoid patterns of
puzzle pieces clinging together
in a funeral monument.

The god of those who love
one another shines in a circular form
like a big bubble until it starts
rolling over picture frames
and doors and becomes
a spinning blade sawing off
unphotographed nights.

The god of the indifferent
appears in a point of infinitesimal
dimension piercing the wall of silence
letting invisible light shoot
through like sand driven
by a desert storm;
eyes can smart and drizzle
even in total darkness.

County Road

When the dark
county road
stands up at night
it doesn't stand
quite erect
but keeps swaying
as if the effort
of standing up straight
had drained it of all
the power of asphalt
and now it's only
the white stripes
on the sides
and the middle
that keep it from
falling back
into the lap
of the night

Twists and Turns of Map Noir

Dead-end alleys
fenced-in parks
non-comprendo grins

twists and turns
not marked
on the sweaty city map

twists and turns that throw
a bucket of lukewarm panic
over your plans

twists and turns though that
can also put the wheels of life
under a strange city

and later replay its unmapped
streets in the bare
desert of the night

Brief Belief

the ocean may splatter its brains
on the shore regularly but the sun
makes a believer of me every evening
when it briefly walks on water

on the red carpet rolled out
between just the two of us
between me and its divine chariot
for a brief luminous spell

while I feel I too could walk
on water and run to this god
begging it to take me along
on its warm and heavy shoulders

rather than leaving me behind
for another night darkened by
demented ghosts squabbling over
my dead footprints in the sand

dead dreams about walking like
the sun on a calm pewter-platter sea
and listening to the waves
with golden but silent nods

The City on the Hill

I.

On the way to Jerusalem we stopped
to take pictures of ourselves under the olive trees
while the sky had withered to a lightless gray;

a winter day grants but a short shrift,
the spirit seeks itself in dark images
and in rocks enshrined in more rocks and glass,

yet the City opened its walls toward us
like welcoming arms
and we stopped again,
turned to sweet salt by the picture of the City on the Hill,
through tear-lenses we fixed the image
that transfixed us
before rushing to its bosom.

2.

On the Hill, memory shines on the Word,
domes and spires are its meaning,
the streets are verses of a psalm,

spiritual debris left behind by pilgrimages past
litter the aisles and altar stones,
the fallout of revelations that exploded long ago
now start secondary explosions

in little hearts seeking solace and a restroom
where to dump the anxieties of the Valley
and the agonies of the Mount;

seek and ye shall find everything
that brought you here
and everything that will drive you home.

The History of Nothing

"I found nothing inside,"
  said the plume-helmeted Roman general,
  stepping out of the Holy of Holies.

"Praise be to God,"
  said the beggar sitting on the Temple steps.
"God made himself invisible just in time."

"But for reasons of security,"
  went on the general, looking back at the Temple,
"we'd better burn it down."

"Yes, my Lord," said the High Priest,
"let flames purify the walls that
  have been desecrated."

"Let's instead erect a statue to Caesar in
  the Holy of Holies," said the beggar.
"These Temple steps are home to me..."

Anyway, the Doves

No one has died yet in the old town
without the blessing of the doves,
they greet the living and departing
with equal fervor and solicitude,

they want to know how you are
and how you propose to solve your problems,
how you believe you can defeat the world
out there where your god has already

condemned you to a frivolous exit and
a stupidly tenacious will to fight it all the way
without even knowing what you're
fighting against or what you're fighting for;

no one has died yet in the old town
without it being observed by the doves
in hallowed songs and hollow tunes,
small things you hear at weddings and

late-morning funerals where the mourners
silently stare at their hands and the doves
have to say it for them: life has a meaning
somewhere, the sky informs us every day.

Frying Pan Morning

a grimy old frying pan
cast-iron dark
dripping with burnt oil
and wielded by a madwoman
with gray hair undulating over the sky

that's how a rainy morning descends
and hits you over the head
with a silent but commanding thud
knocking you out
and leaving you groggy for the rest of the day

that pan is not worth scrubbing clean
might as well chuck it in the trash
and start a new day
with sunny-side up

The Orphan Key

Nothing is more orphan than a key
    without a door to open
        without a lock to welcome and
           embrace it...
a key to a toyota that broke down and got junked
    two years ago
sits in my hand begging for attention,
    whispering in a hoarse
        bashful voice of the time when I had misplaced it
        and turned the whole house upside down in search of it,
how important it was then to me,
    and how
and just how can I now
    toss it in the trashcan?
    Orphans have a right to live
even though belonging to no one,
so what right do I have to play god
    and consign this orphan to its grave?
Or is it perhaps a well-deserved rest,
    a position as important as it was
        to bruise its way into a lock and make it turn?

Insomniac Dreams

The Fat Lady Sings

...but it's not over even after the fat lady sings
if the fat lady is Monserrat Caballé and she sings
mi chiamano Mimi and the fat tenor is Luciano
Pavarotti who sings *che gelida manina* like they did
back in nineteen seventy-six one evening at the Met

when the chandeliers turned into a snowfall of goose bumps
the seats burst into a mellifluous bloom of cheers
every note soared as a star in the extra-dark bohemian night
and the curtain burned up in shame for trying to
put an end to a story that was never to end but go on

carrying the whole house past the slender storyline
of a romance to a special stage where it's not over
when the fat lady sings because when she sings she pours
out the endless strands of a melody and she weaves them
into a love story between Mimi and Rodolfo and more

a love story between the fat lady and Mimi
between the fat singers and the arias glowing on their faces
between the drama and the music
between the tune-drunk audience and the nectar of opera
between the traffic noise of life outside and the music within

because when the fat lady sings everyone who listens
turns into a miniature live opera house where the fat lady
never stops singing and the fat tenor never stops
answering her call and the two of them never stop
becoming younger and more beautiful bohemians every day...

(The poem refers to the opera La Bohème *by Puccini)*

Friday in MOMA with George

(scribbles under an exhibit of drawings by Seurat)

it's like sunday used to be with george in the park
free admission at moma
and now it's george again who takes your hand
on a tour of paris at the fin de siècle

when europe was anchored to huge horse chestnut trees
and it held smokestacks in hand as dirty candles

more often a walk in the park invited a neurotic dusk
and eyes to open in the sky

bare body parts grew on rhododendrons
and enigmatic drapery was dripping from the roof tiles

but of course it was not in the park
but in the outskirts of town in a drizzle of silent soot

silence we have not seen since

the silence of a bicycle being walked

the silence of lovers unwrapping love with their eyes
out on the first and surreptitious date just before curfew

the silence of a seurat drawing behind glass

behind the silence of a shameless freeloader holding
george's hand

behind the silence of an unopened can of sardines

the silence of an unread book an unlived life

any day with george in the dark

Art-Drunk Midnight

fake trees run into fake cars
in front of fake spectators

after midnight when the fake and the real
fight it out for the artist's soul

and a fake moon balloons
across a fake sky

mooning in a dream-drunk masquerade
with the stars dream-waltzing around it

it's only when the moon is
the real thing that it hates being a moon

and loves being a moon, because it knows
there's no difference

even a real moon is fake now and then
and only dreams of being a moon

and starts faking itself
while enjoying the show

an auto-erotic conception and birth

dream-clad nakedness of existence

dream display of awareness
without the merest beam of moonlight

the artist must fake the props of reality
on which to hang his soul

Short Course on Freedom

if you want five fingers on your hand
you're free to have them

if you want four fingers on one hand
you're free to chop one off

if you want six fingers on one hand
you're free to imagine an extra one

freedom is to fill the shape nature gave you
and to find the limits of your soul

freedom is a five-finger exercise but first
you have to let life teach you to count

Macedonian Dreams

the pale shadow i left behind nude
on the art deco tiles of a borrowed bath
as a child

is alive and living in a loving pool
where the two of us can
swim to macedonia

there are no whistles there to stop us
from matriculating under the table

we can go and macerate the gleam
of the bare macedonian tiles
or the shadow of any crevice or muscle we
can offer to the touch of the pool

our smiles can swim into any flexing bump
or opening and rediscover
the lost continent of macedonia

the pool suspends the rules of
the innocence
and forgives the frolics of
our premature efforts at flight

because yes
the child can still grab and hold
onto my forbidden Macedonia

The Trees of Eden

*"When one is one within oneself
one is one with god"* —Ancient proverb

We are all born in eden
but few of us can stay for life,
one by one we wander off
and never find the way back;

wherever one walks in eden,
one is always on a road,
and everything one eats
becomes a sweet ripe fruit,

but outside of eden we cannot walk
without bumping into a tree,
and every fruit we bite into starts
rotting at once, becoming waste,

no wonder we often dream
about life back in eden
and even look for a road
that might lead back there,

but on the way back we keep bumping
into trees that split us in half,
one part made of pain
and the other of dreams,

and the two parts keep bumping
into each other worse than trees.
It is whispered by the leaves
that one can get back into eden

only when one can be one
within oneself and one without;
and that's why one never
bumps into the trees of eden.

Midden of Dreams: Barefoot Flowers

she wore pink-flowered pajamas
and I really didn't believe
she was the angel of death
as she claimed
and I agreed to carry her across 3rd Ave
only because she asked me to
and because she had no shoes on

but when I set her down
on the hood of a Toyota
legally parked by the curb
she suddenly flew off with a smile
saying something like I'll be back

but now I have no idea
how much longer to wait for her
standing here on the sidewalk
next to a wastebasket that reeks of
half-consumed take-out dreams
in Styrofoam wrappings
and I'm not even sure if I have shoes on

Dark Windows in the Fog

Fog in front of me,
fog closing in behind me.
Fog in the middle?

How will I know it
if I drop dead with no one
around to see me?

If a tree could speak
its fall would still be ignored
by the other trees.

Silence rolls ahead,
silence follows on my heels.
A blank line between.

The fog exhaled by
the ground freezes into trees.
I exhale dead songs.

Maybe the fog is
a large crowd stripped of its voice.
Bare souls on display.

Even deer turn gray
on a diet of fog and
stop noticing people.

Fog before me, fog
behind me, fog everywhere.
What's this in my mouth?

Weather-beaten bark
weeping the tears of winter.
Stones sweat in the rain.

Sunset Dives into Lake Balaton

to Elizabeth, in memory of a poetry workshop on the beach

…an upside-down
exclamation mark
drawn by a bored child-god
with a red crayon
on a large pewter platter
still warm from
the hammering of
a broad-faced summer day…

…or a one-line haiku
without words
diving into a blind
one-eyed mirror,
into a looking glass
that does not
look back at
the corroding sky…

The Second Coming of Antichrist

When she takes too much antidepressant
at dusk, Auntie Anne,
lying back on her Victorian sofa,
tends to see Antichrist
climb over the antimacassar
toting his taut anti-crucifix.

She calls out to him: Antichrist!
Antichrist!
Praying for an anticlimax has worn me out,
but I'll do it,
if you really want to come again!

The Eighth Dwarf

not short enough to be one of them
not tall enough to make it in the outside world
not even napoleon size
the eighth dwarf
more like a sulking child with a Halloween mask

after the business agent dropped him from the act
the other seven let him hang around for a while

but when the picayune packs of missing cash
went from dribbles to wads
they sent him off to rehab

and only paid his rent and grocery bills
but not gambling debts or the pushers

his letters to Snow White were thrown away
by her press agent

his calls to the Wicked Witch were never returned

he was too wicked for one
and not wicked enough for the other

finally the eighth dwarf wrote his own storybook
with lots of dirt on the others

but the unagented book only managed to collect
a few rejection slips and only from small presses

there was too much social criticism for fiction and
the lies were not outrageous enough for a true story

now he has a spot off Times Square where for a pint bottle
he's willing to entertain foreign tourists

at least he's short enough not to hurt himself badly
when he falls down drunk

Monosyllabic Words

they are the pits in the lush flesh of language
the hard-bitten monosyllabic words

good   black   love   death   crib

the man in the street spits them out with gusto
but lawyers and theologians carefully avoid them
lest they choke on them or get lost in the street

white   sky   sex   bad   life

slip past the tongue before it can savor them
before it can attach a song to them

red   bold   blood   fear   gay

flash by before the teeth can forge them into a chain
to capture that inner monster
and lead it out on the page without taming it

flesh   hot   flesh   cold   flesh   sick

monosyllabic words are only there if they march
in a row and row after row pounding the ground
shouting that the dragon is awake

Costume Drama in the Nude

(Additional Frames)

The day the swords melt
in the hands of the gallant duelers
the overturned picnic tables
stagger back to their feet,
goblets hop back from the grass
and pewter platters of chicken legs
sail in on the tables
with carnations marching right
into the pot in the middle
while flags ooze out of tall
erect poles supported by
iridescent weeds of merriment....

The swords melt but the fray
takes on a new tone in another key:
the duelers begin to cross their tongues
and parry with their lips
their arms clinging to each other's
spastic dance
to the din ringing in chewed-off ears
and eyes drooling with saliva—

scenes like this do not just fade out
but become another heave
in the lungs of the Uni-Verse.

Rat Factory

A headache rattling
in a rickety rat-poisoned
rat factory

where did you leave
your footsteps
but inside your skull

between your ears where
rats run a ratcheting old
rat refectory

rat-size headache nibbling
on a rat-made
poisoned rat factory

factory-ache
brick-ache
window-ache

open the window
and look at the ache
in the rickety rackety rat factory

just look at the rat-ravaged ache
tugging and teasing it
into a rocketing rat ache

a factory ache
where rats are made
to eat the ache

and to poison a
rat-poison warehouse
a rattling old rat factory

where headaches roll
from wall to wall
kicked by ratty rats

like a cubic ball that
wants to eat the rats and bats and
the rickety rackety rat factory hats

Belgian Still Life Without Canvas

Rhododendrons stumble closer
to the windows at suppertime

they put on scary masks and
funny ones too but we inside
have to guess which is which

whether to hide the carving knife
or else raise our glasses toward
the windows before the masks
can turn the blood to wine
and the wine to blood

but on the silver platter
the innocently pinkish flesh
has already stopped wiggling
and so we must proceed
with the meal

lest the rhododendrons
march through the white villa
and take the supper with them
leaving behind only pebbles of blood
on the damask and the curtain of
our empty stares in the window

The Grand Bazaar

the vaulted temple
was lit by flames
blinking from brown
immovable eyes

the bronze statue said
the carpet could fly
and take me places
mentioned in fables

but the camels woven
into the pattern looked
skeptical and far from
ready for the sky

Tightrope Too

It's all right to be naked if you're standing
on a tightrope while singing Lucia's
mad scene, juggling the coloratura notes,

and the people passing by below you pay no
attention as they go about their business,
pushing and shoving and lugging their cares,

while you're up there, bouncing the notes
till they all are caught in a rainbow and
your nakedness is discovered by a breeze.

An Idol Not Cruel

the artisan's knife should be sharp but
not cruel like a straight razor
only sharp like the outlines of the image
you want to carve out of a block
of wood

and the wood should yield to every
well-directed cut
but deflect those that would go
too deep

the cuts should be bold in the beginning
but then gradually become gentler
and smaller
until finally they barely touch
the burnished skin

the block of wood
should be from the tree of life in Eden
even if it has to be cut down
for the creation of that face

and the finished idol should
come alive
and plant a new tree of life
in an Eden always freshly grown

Wozzeck Paraphrases

(on the tracks of Georg Büchner and Alban Berg)

The crimson glare of the moon nails me
to the knife, but whose hand is gripping
the throat of this evening?
Blood seeps out of the sting crimped
by the new earrings,
gold bleeds on guilty cheeks,
but whose cheeks can I touch
if not Marie's? She's touched my eyes once,
how could I see anything else but her?
The knife stabs my fist, I can feel its grin
gleaming through the curtain of the night,
I can feel its blade arching from her pillow
to the bloodied moon,
but the moon's trinkets had to go,
I had to tear them off her face,
the only way to stop the boots
of that oompah music from marching
over my bed and over the cheeks
that once were as close to me as the moon...
If I open my fingers those cheeks, those eyes,
will fall into the pool of the night...

Violent Concerto No. 1

By the end of the first movement
the violin virtuoso finishes sawing
through his instrument
and he's free to swish the bow
over the orchestra...

first, he slices off a hand
and then heads start to roll,
the bow slashes and cuts
a swath through the players
adding red to the black and white
color scheme
until finally the conductor alone is
left there standing;
he parries the bow
with his baton
on the initial attack
but then he stumbles
off the podium,
and the bow gets him in the jugular
with the audience
adding the final coda
in a roaring ovation.

But it's not over yet;
then the players stagger to their feet
spraying blood into the house
which results in a frenzy of celebration,
the chandelier comes crashing down,
the untethered roof takes off like a balloon,
lifting the walls with it...

why else is it so quiet when
the ushers slam the doors shut
on a concert hall?

Chamber Opera in Ten Acts

(With One-Year Intermissions)

1. I don't recall what happened then,
   we probably just went home.

2. Don't hang me on an xmas tree,
   I cannot glow with a carol in my mouth.

3. It was cold then and it's cold now,
   but then it had a better story.

4. We don't hold the door open for the night...
   it catches up with us just as we reach out...

5. We'll never again set foot in her kitchen
   while the drunken grin of fall embraces the clock...

6. Of course, summer too slobbered its
   warm soup of tears on our sunglasses.

7. No more was said on the subject...
   silence walked us home in heavy boots.

8. Once I was tempted to touch a pair of lips,
   but luckily words got there first.

9. A message almost landed on me once...
   I died on the spot and started doing the dishes.

10. We went home before the show ended,
    and we don't go out any more...
    the night comes to visit us almost twice daily.

Insomniac Dreams

(inside Francis Bacon's paintings)

What do they say
the chunks of flesh
to the darkness
hugging them?

Black is alive
with hidden colors
while light lacks
the depth of black.

Close the windows
turn out the light
undress the night and bathe
your bareness in it.

Light is only alive
when it punches you out
and you lie flat on
your face staring into
a deep dark crack,

and your flesh starts to
howl at the bloody cage
of light for the comforting
hand of a big black night.

The Country of the Soul

The Last Wind and the Last Man on Earth

after the last man finally devours
               the next to the last man
he'll stalk out into the desert
and the city will finally come to a standstill
streets and avenues will come to a halt
lights will go off and never go on again
streetcars will sink into the street
parked cars will turn into curbstones
bricks will grow over windows and doors
               like skin over wounds
grass will grow over rooftops like fur on sheep
silence will grow a silver tree and spread an airy and
               tinkling canopy that may not even be there
it may just be that the wind will finally have
               a chance to stop and think
because winds stop long before eating the last wind

The War's Unfinished Nocturne

the escaping roof tiles of
the bombed-out burning temple
explode all around my bed
and I wonder if it was a dream
or a war

looking back into the night
I see nothing but the dark
and hear only the explosions
of bloodied stained-glass windows
the bang-bang of
my footsteps trying to run away

but it's so hard to step out
of the acrid smoke of fear
and run blind back to bed

to clutch the hand a new day
extends to you
if you can pull the white flag
of surrender over your head

if you can remember the prayer
you massacred long ago
but these words are not
even its bones
not even its broken tiles
not its scratching fingernails

Armistice Day Parade

On the Boulevard de l'Opéra
the battle lines are drawn
by the baroque and faux renaissance façades
of the deluxe apartment houses,
and the battlefield is the wide boulevard between them;
at first light in the morning
the front lines start their advance toward each other,
bricks and cornices are lobbed at the advancing edifice,
doors slam shut but windows pop open and spray
shards of glass across the narrowing gap and,
finally,
just before the two sides crash
the balconies get pulverized
and the window ornaments explode into dust
and then the grinding force of the impact
heaps a rising crescendo of the rumble
ground out by the heavy structures;
for a moment the walls flatten face to face: bang!
then there is the low moan of walls giving way,
collapsing over each other,
but it's not over while there is still one wall standing,
for what stands up must keep on the move
until it's tripped by the rubble;
but once it's over peace returns,
the bricks and stones struggle back to their places
in the walls facing each other
across the busy boulevard,
to wait for the next signal
at another dawn.

Free Ride

From an office window it's hard to follow
the pilgrim's path through the torrents of cables
in a petrified concrete forest; only he can see
the path that rolls out in front of his sneakers.

Now and then he waves from the ribbon of
weeds racing along the railroad tracks; no thanks,
he doesn't need a thing. The scanty smile of his
beard says his feet give him a free ride, and

he has already arrived at his destination:
the pilgrimage. He wishes the best to those
he left behind, to those who still hope to
sprout new leaves and shout fresh blooms

like the weeds he greets with a message:
they too are free and on a pilgrimage, and
if they don't care where they're going
they'll find a path molded to their feet.

I'd follow him, but my third-floor sealed windowpane's
between us, and so are my eyes. I could buy an Amtrak
ticket or hop in my car and beat him, but where? No car
can take me where he's going, where I'd rather be.

Postcard from Budapest

(remembering the Saltus Danubius epidemic after WWII)

The Danube bends irresolutely as if
trying to stretch and shake off
the temptation to fall asleep

like the lions holding up the bridge,
granite eyes unblinking,
refusing ever to bark

at the cars feeding the bridge or at
a homeless man trying to trip the tourists
with his leg bones sticking out,

but the splash doesn't stop the river
from stretching, doesn't set off
the lions or pop the blue blister
of the sky; the bridge can connect
worlds much farther apart
than Buda and Pest;
it leaps all the way back to the starving
war survivors who leaped into a river
even hungrier than they were.

Tales from the Trap

Dead mice do tell tales,
their voices burrow deeper
in your head than did their
claws in the attic; your
soul is the trap where their
voices will be stuck forever
like the mangled furry mess
now on the little plastic tray,
garnished with poop that
popped out in the struggle
to gnaw off the captured foot,
now just a bloody stub still
stuck and pointing at you
louder than the open jaws
now resting, finally, on
the cushion of a tale you'll
have to whisper to the garbage
can and say it wasn't you who
did it;
it takes a giant to make
a bloody mess
of that captive-crappy little life,
a giant whose tale will crush
right through the ceiling
right above your bed.

Feelings

How does a god feel when
trees and bushes turn green
without asking for his blessing?

How does a tree feel
when its leaves start turning pale?

How do the pale leaves feel when
the tree starts letting go of them?

How does a breeze feel
when a lull stops it in its tracks?

How does a star feel when
being slowly snuffed out by dawn?

How does a window feel when night comes
and it has nothing to show outside?

How does a door feel when
there's no one to keep out?

How does a car feel with the hood up
standing idle by the road?

How does a page feel left blank?

How does a bird feel high in the sky
on suddenly forgetting how to fly?

How does a fish feel
about the world above the surface?

How does a pen feel when words
walk off the page and fly unaided
over a puddle of eyes and ears?

How does a feeling feel
in a paralyzed breast
running out of sighs?

What Finality Feels Like

the leaves do not abandon a tree just
because it's broken
knocked down by a summer storm

they may turn brown but will hang on
even when the leaves of other trees
still standing
start jumping overboard in droves
taking refuge in the loam

so that in the spring they can sneak
back in the tree and up to their perch
on the branches for another season

but the leaves of a dead tree have
no place to go
they might as well hang on
and wait for the end of the world

until the steel monsters clear out the forest
for another Walmart parking lot

but then the leaves with season passes too
will learn what finality really feels like

Inside, Outside in the Jungle

A full glass wall makes
the schoolroom a safe
harbor of sunshine.

Green waves of foliage lap the glass
testing the invisible border
between inside and outside.

Suddenly the jungle
opens machine-gun fire.
Parakeets join in.

A tiger with a bandolier
across the shoulders
turns his snarl at the class

and commands us
to tell him
which side we're on.

On the winning side,
roars out the class as one,
except my mouth is full.

Whose balls are you chewing?
demands the tiger,
ready to charge at me,

and I can already
see him bite into my groin,
leaving me naked.

Very naked is indeed
the one who hasn't got
a side to be on.

The Ratgod

What the fires don't eat the rats will,
the ashes and the blessing hand of the pope;
rats attend the biggest mass in history,
whether black or otherwise,

and that's because their god is not one huge,
enormous rat that creates and eats up all the other rats
but the amorphous mountain
made of the rat population,

the tumbling and fumbling dust cloud of
sniffing noses and scrambling feet and arching backs,

it's a god that's so easy to see and worship,
a religion so temptingly simple;
your sin becomes the sin of your god,
you can gnaw on children's juicy fingers
and procreate in the subway tunnels
running thru the basement of saint patrick's

and it's all in your god's name,
for you are but a hair on his enormous belly,
the unholy communion of rats,
you cannot lose: even in death you grow,

your god can feed on the dead,
on the garbage you craft with your teeth,
on the shadows you leave behind.

The City Wind

The uncouth city wind tears in
restlessly to rattle all the windows
but rails only at the brightly lit;
its curses crawl up on the bare
bricks, walls can't stop the shiver
as the wind staggers down the alley,
tossing trash cans on the naked
belly of the avenue and pasting wet
newspapers against defenseless
shop doors. But if you listen long enough
you start to make sense of the ravings;
they're not against the light
or the silence spilling from the windows
but against their slow
line of immobility,
that's what the city wind
has to rattle and shake.

Pedestal City Revisited

the statues of the old god are
long gone now
pulled down and melted down
into cannons and storm bells

the revolution has re-made
the city in its own image
barricades and barbed wire have
replaced bronze and marble

but a hardy variety of the shadow
cast by the old god's statues
keeps on growing among the ruins
especially at night

and now the horses of the one-time
rebels are seen out there
grazing on the shadows and even
the watchdogs join in the feast

Dona Mihi Pacem

a man of peace decides
to show his city
what war is like

he forms a one-man
execution squad
and shoots himself

but the mortar fire
on the tv screens
drowns out the shot

so he hangs himself from
the outstretched sword of
a stone general in central park

but the flags flying
around the statue
cover up his rope

then this man of peace
douses himself with
gasoline in times square

and puts a match to this torch
but the savvy critics declare
the show an instant hit

and a smart agent starts
selling the flames
to tourists for souvenirs

and exhibits the man
of peace in a glass cage
as a real-life terrorist

The Taste of Blood

Red-hot peppers come
pretty close but play
a poor second
to the taste of blood

whose warmth
floods your palate
with the comfort
of easy victory

over the big bite
you've taken from
the barely cooked flesh
flushed with red blood

but then comes the heat
of a sneak attack
the enemy's all over
your mouth and your guts

and it's too late to spit
it out or wash it down
with the wine of slogans
too late even to moan

the taste of blood flows
over the sting of pepper
over any spice
nature can throw at you

it kills its source first
in the sacrificial lamb
and then it kills your taste
for anything but blood

The Sweet Stink of Money

The stink of money is glitter and music
to those who swim in its waves
as it goes cascading through
streets and malls and even chic new
restaurants ruled over by power-hungry
steaks, their tepid backsides basted
in the mud baths of brandy sauce...

The stink is glitter and glissando
waving its way around the cornerstones
of quiet banks and modish bazaars,
navigated by the red sails of SALE signs
and compounded interest quotations,
the stink is human and the waste is
immortal in its majestic flow,

the stink is glitter that tickles the nose
and crawls down the palate
like a drunken monk into the cellar
to fetch another pitcher of wine,
but he's too befuddled to see what
comes out of the tap; the stink is a love
potion for the love of death...

On Exhibit

The carnival social life:
a leper colony or a museum?
We cannot decide just what we want;
exhibit our wounds or genitals,
or both at once?

We lift our naked shirts and drop our pants,
but when someone sneers at our wounds
we begin to wiggle our groins
and bleed profusely every time
there's a giggle about our nakedness.

The lights are turned on and off, but
we're afraid of going home;
even the potted palms are
fighting depression in the lobby
but refuse to flap back to a shore.

Once in a while two exhibits might
bump into each other
and a buzz of excitement foams up
on the high-tech nickel staircase:
what's it gonna be?

Who knows? No one can tell pus
from sperm here anymore; blood and ketchup are
miscegenating and the result is just another exhibit,
something to lay down on black velvet and let
it show its swelling wounds and festering genitals.

But business is slow; no one's even looking
when there's so much to show.

Two-Sided Mistake

Two hands were given to man so that they
    may work together in an uneasy alliance;
while one is extended in supplication
    the other gives the world the finger;
while one leg is bended to kneel
    on the slippery road to heaven
the other kicks an ass, a stomach,
    a groin or a soul;
while one eye seeks out the god
    that has made him live
the other looks for a way to fix
    that god's mistakes;
while one ear hears
    the alarms of the end
the other strives to scoop up
    the sweetness of fairy tales;
but man was given only one tongue
    with which to shovel out
the truth and lies in one
    promiscuous flow of hymns.

Bombs in Armchairs

Fire doesn't cleanse the house,
soot only thickens the grime.
Truth dressed in smoke soon
sours and pokes fun at its worshipers.

Ruins house no one very comfortably,
not even fire.

A bullet does not insert love
into a loveless heart and the bad news
it brings is somewhat belated.

A lie can be dwarfed only by a bigger lie,
and their struggles trample
truth into the mud.

One bomb in hand is worth two
you have already defused.
Keep working.

Tickets to the show offend those who lack them,
but stopping the show will not increase
the number of seats in the theatre.

Stop throwing bombs from your armchair,
the upholstery might explode under you,
and you'll have to live with you own stench
burning through the rest of your chairbound years.

Fire cannot build Utopia,
but it can bake bricks, the building blocks
of the new world you preach about.

Silence versus Noise

Silence is mute standing before Noise,
there's no escape;
the sharp notes may cause an itch,
but the soul can be quietly scratched
unless Noise happens to
bang its fist on it;

Silence kowtows but not
all the way to the ground where Noise's
alligator shoes hammer away;

what's Silence to do?
Close the windows and doors?
Noise knocks a hole and reaches in,
its square jaw snapping at Silence,
its sharp eyes nailing Silence to the wall;

let Silence be silent here
where only Noise is allowed to speak
and roar
because space and time belong to Noise,
be it a room or a city square,
morning or night,
they all belong to Noise
even the chapel Silence built into its own skull;

not only all words but all pictures,
all billboards, wall space and all monitor screens
of the world are in the hands of Noise,
and so are all pulpits and all judges' gavels;

Silence has learned to be satisfied with
its mere existence,
for it exists at the pleasure of Noise
mostly in broken TV sets and rusty wrecks
like a shy violet growing in an illegal dump.

But violets will keep growing even after the last com-
mand of that final crescendo.

The Country of the Soul

"...at the skin my being doesn't end."—*George Faludy*

A porous organic fence built not only for defense but as
an explorer of the unknown and an envoy to the familiar;
antenna and transmission tower: the skin.

That's the border of the country of being, but being
doesn't have to stop there if the border guards let
the soul slip in and out on the waves of the universal wing;

where are you now? Still hiding in your skin?
The outside stops where you hang your skin curtain,
but it doesn't have to be of iron, does it?

Teased by the fingertip lights of life it becomes
tight and you're ready to jump out of it;
but if life throws teardrops at your skin,
are you willing to step out and ask why?

Better yet, just ask how? Reach out and ask how
you can help to stop the flow of tears; but even better
yet, show there's life beyond the skin; beyond
the pain and pleasure, that's where life begins.

Let your being step beyond the skin.

From a Hiker's Diary

Hiking the Canada Dry Trail

its two-liter belly so empty
it could take off like a balloon
from the trailside

only ninety-nine cents
since nineteen oh four
Canada Dry bottle

wild cherry soda
artificially and
naturally flavored

red label on clear plastic
red enough to cut the small brook's
rock-plaqued artery

red enough to torture
my eyes before biting them
and I almost stumble into

a six-foot black snake
slithering across the trail
without though biting me

but it tells me to pick up
that empty red invader
even if it's not my trash

at the trailhead I have no
choice but dump both myself
and the bottle into my car

and then dump the car
into the Interstate
sewer of traffic

Trail to Timelessness

the month of may snakes silently
through the bend of the old logging trail
two or three county roads away

from the interstate in a PA game land
where the loudest thing is a cricket
in the sun-silenced grass of the hillside

and the fastest is a yellow oak leaf sailing
on a lazy creek among the rocks
or perhaps the fuzzy caterpillar by my boots

both are faster than the single-engine plane above
that wants to stop there and freeze into the sky
like an insect immortalized in blue amber

Springing

daffodils tower over
the murmuring residues
of hoary winter tales

their stalks scratch the naked
breeze and claw her
billowing giddiness

flocks of yellow static
skip over the clearing
without ever disappearing

the sun drinks up the air but
the dregs it leaves behind turn into
little black flies in your ears and eyes

while you stand there trampling
on the skeletons of last year's weeds
waiting for the daffodils
to call you their long-lost kin

Morning Metamorphosis

if god is good then dead
dogs fall from the sky
       I opened my eyes that morning
to find one lying by my bed
head tucked under broken legs
and naked belly exposed to the fading darkness
       I closed my eyes quickly again
and tried to go back to sleep
but the dog's plaintive silence
rang in my ears
       the traffic noise was murmuring from far away
but how long does it take to get hit by a car?
       I pressed my eyelids shut
but in the self-imposed darkness
I began to feel as exposed as the dog
no longer in bed but in the middle of the street
and as ugly as a dead dog
       that cannot get back on its feet
so I had to lie there
waiting for another car to run over me
and then another
perhaps a garbage truck
       until my body was flattened against the pavement
only a thin layer of organic matter
with even the flies and the eyes dead and flattened out
exposed to the sun
the wind
the dissipating power of nature
       and then I'd be blown away as dust
a small cloud of dust
that could steal back into my bed
       and wake up again staring at my bathrobe
crumpled on the floor
       looking like a dead dog that will never
have to open its eyes again
on that morning or ever
if god is good

Stealing Mountains

I take my mountains for a walk
stolen mountains amassed between
the trail and taking a deep breath

stolen mountains camouflaged
under thick green blankets of whining
under the hazy glaze of distance

stolen mountains gluing up my eyes
spraying my chest with sweat
and sprinkling the breeze with fleas

stolen mountains sitting and listening
to every lie I tell
every prayer I've forgot

should be grateful for little favors
but I am busy trying
to imagine the world without me

while others walking their dogs are
busy trying to imagine an unimaginable
god pulling the strings

behind stolen mountains
he has stolen from another god
even more unimaginable

something is bound to spring up
and stir up the dark green sky
something to fatten the light

stolen mountains break up
into infinitesimal infelicities
and invade the bloodstream

watered-down blood cascades
over the rocks of our scattered curses
the bony knees of a solid god

Mount Minsi

On reaching the top I round a cliff
to wipe the sweat off my glasses and
then pray to a god I had left below
somewhere under a book by Barbusse
or Voltaire, but I just have to ask someone
if I am for real
and anyone will do...
I keep talking about the fall colors piling up
on the hillside,
life for miles in front of me glories in its
last burst of self-assertion before the end...

So, what's this show of colors for?
Maples, oaks and poison ivy
vying with one another in extravagant display
and it's all for nothing,
it's not to attract a mate or life-giving pollen
carried by bees and other flying friends,
not to initiate a new phase of life;
it's a game Nature plays with herself
in a luscious onanistic orgy—
the golden leaves bask in their own beauty
with unabashed self-gratification;

they don't care if their life is lapped up
by the big gray-bearded sky...

Before she dies, Nature becomes a selfish
god who hoards riots of pleasure and takes them to the grave,
a god who's got nothing to lose
by going crazy with drunken colors...

And I, too, begin to feel red spots
burned into my cheeks...

Squirrel Gods

They're always busy chewing
on the passing moment they grab
from a bottomless hole of the present
with their immortal claws.

For them the present never ends,
I've never seen a squirrel
without its jaws grinding away
on an endless point in time;

for them the present never runs out,
and so for them there is no future,
no death, no fear of death and
no need for a god to protect them;

being immortal, they are gods,
and even when you hit one
on the road, it doesn't die,
only stops chewing, while you

still grope at the robes of death
in a dark chapel of your mind,
calling on a god to come
and turn on the light.

A Night at the Opera

it's like an unfamiliar opera
in a foreign tongue
yet I listen spellbound
to the bird songs of the sunset
in my front-row box seat
on the back porch

I cannot tell you what
this opera is all about
but I can understand every word
while it's on
while I sit on my imaginary wings
and listen to the free performance

there are no super- or subtitles
no simultaneous translation
I only have to open an inner ear that
the daytime world plugs up
and I can tune in to nature's tongue
I can understand not only the world
but even myself in it
and forgive us both

Immortality Denied

the end is near
my basil plant feels it
and tries desperately to escape
by leaping into the next generation
every day now it tries to bolt
but a cruel god keeps breaking off
the budding tips
the fetal flowers
he keeps torturing the plant
to get a few more leaves out of it
before summer withers and
the exhausted plant collapses
without leaving progeny behind

Brooklyn Bat

The robin doesn't care if he's in Brooklyn or
Hoboken. Is the C train running on express tracks
today? It's not weekend yet, Thursday,
isn't it? Unless the week is running late
like the C train, if it's running at all.

The rails are steeling themselves, already
racing straight into the black bowels of
the city except it's always night
in the subway, but climbing up to the street
doesn't guarantee awakening.

The robin's wings too are on fire or
painted crimson, the color of something
alive, but in the gullet of the tunnel
it still looks more like a bat. Shafted
in an undigested coal mine

Trans Gypsy Moth

The liveliest creature of the summer night,
the gypsy moth, why does it want to
dissolve into a heap of nameless eggs on the bark of an oak?

Does a gypsy moth remember being a cocoon? Or a caterpillar?

And as a caterpillar, feasting on delicious oak leaves,
why does it want to turn into a cocoon?
Does it know it's the way to gain the freedom of flight?
Does it know it really wants to be a moth and lay eggs and why?
Does it root fiercely for next year's swarm of gypsy moths?

Does it hope they will sing the same hymn they're now
reveling in? The one that gives them a lift in the air,
makes them attack the screen door
and bang on it with the demand for existence?

I remember being an abandoned farm house
in an open field with not even a dirt trail leading to it.

I can also see myself as a logging road in a fall forest,
my hair the color of a gypsy moth.

Canyon Dreams

Only in mile-deep silence do
red rocks flex their muscles and
scale the walls to watch the virgin
chasm crying out between them;

the sky overflows with blue
well-rehearsed harmonies,
but the pillars soak up
the excess chords along with those

who come here to listen to
the color of red rocks and seek
their powerful embrace: flesh
no matter how hard it speaks

is only flesh flexed and open
and ready to be sacrificed
to the heavy shadows discarded
like pods by the rising pillars,

they stand and fall with the blue
rhythms of the sky; sweat blends
into those who get lost down here
and makes them grow as cliffs.

Birds of Different Feather

The game is familiar, almost innocuous,
people's names get away from me
and hide behind the grin of their owners.
But I do wish I knew birds by name;

just now I saw three birds of different colors
in the yew outside the bathroom window,
one red, one brown, and the third one blue,
somewhat larger and more stand-offish,

but they all flocked to the same bush
even though they were not
of the same feather,

and I was dying to ask them how
they were getting along together.
But I didn't know their names.

Summer Evening Sonatina

the shadow cast by the poplar branch
hanging over the lawn
seems no wiser than any other creature
at dusk
the blades of grass still have their green
uniforms on
but already half asleep
fireflies move in
and start sketching out the outlines of
the approaching night
on their cue the birdsongs die off
but the ballgame next door marches
across the fence
a home run crashes the window of silence

Drunken Deer Eyes

still warm boletus-brown
and unblinkingly alive
they hit every passing car

but still deny the pain
in the legs that buckle
getting up again and again

she goes down holding
her head high like a tipsy lady who
tries to maintain her dignity

the forest used to be
only a skip from the road
why now so far away

her eyes ask the car-clad passersby
what's happening to me
what's this heavy load

Discovery of the Sky

fall winds falling break up
the green clouds of summer
and open up the brittle
countenance of the sky

colorless skeletons
crowd around the house
carrying a robust blanket
of a hymn balanced

on their cold heavenward
fingertips but sometimes
the dense roar thins out into
the mere scrim of a song

Summer's Throat

Pray for prey
sing the frogs with throats
wide open dark tunnels of love
pray for plenty of prey
and then pray for successful
digestion of their souls
in heaven's belly and bowels
heaven-bound the prey
can't help it but pray
for an open skin to sting
and pump for blood
what does a mosquito know
about the frog and the tunnel of love?
Less than the frog knows
about the beaks airborne above
herons and storks and egrets
What do they pray for
if not for prey?
And who listens to all this praying
and preying and braying?
Nature is a demented mother
made pregnant by these prayers
fecundity lavishly endows
her bed with prey and hunger
and hunger with prey
all that live are prey to her
the deep-throated summer

Sudden and Reckless Peace

the approaching train
heavy going yes
but not if you want to stay
standing on the track
not if you look the engine
straight in the headlights
like deer do on the road

is that playacting I wonder
or the thrill of wrestling
with sudden and reckless peace

grandstanding playacting
call it what you will but
at the end the end will win
no matter who blinks first

From a Hiker's Diary

Take the steepest trail if you want to be sure of getting there,
a downhill trail can only take you back to the car; when hawks
are flying closer to the ground spring must be tickling the wind.

Do not step on a smooth rock when it's wet, even if it lies level
with the ground; the other side of the sun shines even brighter
and grows bigger boulders.

Do not set a foot between two rocks; even barns take a bow
before they collapse.

Do not step on a root that looks like a snake; the broken arms
of the oak hold the tatters of summer, and I wear her painted
tears in my pocket, in a tissue ball.

Don't believe your legs, they're not in real pain until they
crumple under you and start telling stories about you to the
rocks; the defrocked cardinal is looking for fig leaves behind
the altar, his pudgy hands fall short of his pudenda.

Keep walking until you hear the snow crunch under your feet
or the loam give out a low moan now and then. Listen to them,
but keep going. Even the deer take the marked trail sometimes.

What's this? the Paris metro system? Brooklyn? the copper-
mine trail you never found? Forget the maps; getting lost is the
ultimate destination, life's promise and fulfillment. When
you're lost, you're there and you know it.

Let the zealots munch on their slogans; keep on walking.
Humans too are part of Nature, no less, no more; you too have
the right to tread the trail as much as the deer or gypsy moths
or lightning. *Mors est quies viatoris.*

The end is now: *Quies donatur viatoris, finis est omnis lavoris.* If
you can't cease to wax poetic even when out of breath, remember
there is another peak right after death, or at least another cliff that
hugs the sky. *Quod erat demonstrandum.*

Any water tastes better than what drips from your brow unless it's rainwater. Or snow. Loneliness has a statue in a richly decorated room without walls or roof where the doors are always locked. If you knock twice on the white enameled panels a few notes from a piano will call you in.

Give up? It's too late. Being on the trail you've given up already; now you have to face what remains. This is not a trail, it's a crack in the ceiling; these are not your feet but cockroaches running from the light. And you're watching them with a spray can in hand.

Wild Vase Poetry

The Implanted Epitaph

I wear my tombstone in my chest,
heavy with an epitaph.
It must be true, because it can
make me cry and make me laugh.

I must lug this heavy burden
no matter how heavily it hangs,
carrying it through long years
of sour meals with lonely pangs

of loss over a life consisting
of nothing but one long delay,
a blind date with death that has me
getting ready every day

for one long trip that never starts
yet never ever sees its end;
its destination is a secret
I'm not allowed to comprehend,

a punishment deep in my chest
as well as a sin I must commit
by my atoning for the pain
of reliving and revealing it.

Armageddon Again

Bury me with the rest when it is over
Don't try to look for me in the debris
Names will mean so little to a bulldozer
It will not stop and start looking for me

Bury me under the tread marks of winners
Those still left standing and rushing to claim
Victory's well-deserved ashes as golden
Ornament to their own blood-polished fame

Bury me with the books and the old pictures
Of the museums still burning to know
Who was it started this unholy mess
Whose blood is searing the nuclear snow

Bury the weapons of daily destruction
With my corpse guarding their innocent rust
Let the tanks cover me for I'll be a bomb
Blowing up all that's left with my disgust

Bury me quietly when it is over
I don't want prayers or songs flown above
By anyone else but your bloody bulldozer
Tramping my mass grave before you sign off

Laconic Bulls

some say bulls are fighting my butterflies
in the warmish snow of my bed
but the sword is still held high
and allowed to freely and sweetly sweat

that's the scene you pay to see
in the theatre of the absurd
housed in the shade of an apple tree
clothed with the song of a songless bird

you wish you could get silk wings gored
by butterflies in a puddle of joy
bad luck though you can't find your sword
you have nothing but your tongue to employ

it's the butterflies you're supposed to lick
and sing laconic bull wings with a full throat
catching their hymn just in the nick
of time before it outgrows your coat

when bulls are fighting butterflies
there's nothing else for you to do
but unbind the tricky clock that ties
you to the horn of an impromptu

The Hero of My Childhood

He had a profile made to cleave the wind,
eyes that burned a hole in any guile,
cruel lips that so carelessly sinned
even while curled around an easy smile,

a chin no friend or foe could withstand,
a nose that could've chopped down a tree,
fall colored, wavy hair without a strand
ever out of place or flying free;

even in a classroom or a bar
he seemed to have with him a motorbike,
a biplane, or a pair of skis to ride;

we shook hands, and now there isn't a star
that since then we haven't made our own
or a city sky in which we haven't flown.

The Show: Sex in the Ice Age

Mastodons and mandolins
in the hands of hairy hills
mastodons and a single
time-encrusted mandolin
dressed in the dust of loneliness
which will make her phosphoresce
in the UV light of the moon...

Why did we leave our footprints behind,
why be so mean, so picayune
when we could be riding on
the hairy back of a mastodon,
perched on erectly curling tusks
with our songs dancing on the strings
of an undulating mandolin,

yes, we could be scrubbing
skin on skin,
mastodon and mandolin,
pickled by the burning snow
in the song-shaped, shallow hills,
the silence of the ice-age singing
in the cunning old ravine

before it steals the spotlight
from the mastodon's cold
mandolin.

Still Life in a Shattered Mirror

There's no room for the heady breath
of a rose in the mirror where
the slender neckline of a tulip grows,
or is it courting death to stop the dance

and shatter that glacial shadow with
a never-ending, never-telling glance?
Can the mirror's clatter plug
the still life into life's great grid?

When the tulip lets out its thorns,
blood blooms in sinuous gasps of joy,
when the rose undresses there is
nothing more to grow, nor to destroy,

but when they see each other shimmer
closer in the mirror for a kiss
there's nothing more to thorn,
no more thorny cracks to miss;

a new death is born to this pair
who nurture more than what there is,
a headier and redder breath
in their nectar of despair.

In Sun's Shadow

Even the sun turns its back to me,
and I crawl in its shadow like
a penny left to roll toward the sewer,

a miniature unicycle bike,
a toy made by grown-up gods
for spoiled, stupid children gods,

a joke that barely produces
lukewarm smirks or lazy nods;
sunlight only comes to me

reflected by people's ice-cube eyes,
that's how the sun surveys me
even as it multiplies,

no one has to look for me, I am
just there, in everybody's way,
my wounds and welts, my tearful sins

and tortures on indecent display,
no matter how I try to cover up,
rolling like a lost bad penny to

the cracks of this asphalt universe,
with a smile painted black and blue.
Yet the sun knows where to find me

and how, its back turned toward me sends
its bullets from eyes around me to rape
my every pore, my naked sentiments.

There's no safety or restful peace
in lurking in the shadow of the sun;
I'm dead already, yet the travesty

of my life has just barely begun.
Sometimes though a passing penny
rolls along and shares a tale with me.

Winter Dead

The driveway is under attack
by dark spots that grow
into tumors in the flabby
sick-white body of snow.

Winter is dying and goes
digging its own grave
in the night of the ground
and now nothing will save

its deadly white skin even
if god were to call a halt
and order an investigation
as to who was at fault...

Poetry Paraphrase

The poet carries with him his own forest fire
set ablaze by an objectless desire
as he directs his restlessly metric feet
to an unmapped journey he must complete.

His only way out is to go up in smoke,
sneak into the sky and up there invoke
the freedom of birds and flying insects,
that's the story his poetry reflects.

Every poem is a smoke signal sent
into the human forest in a sacrament,
not an alarm to the fire brigade
but neither is it oil on the fire laid

to gather in a crowd of adoring eyes;
the torch of poetry is not a disguise,
the poet only roams his own forest fire
to find a name for his object of desire.

A poem is a fancy fault in the crust
of everyday life and therefore a must;
it's a forest we may never enter,
yet its call can put us in its center.

A Variation on a Theme by Verlaine

("Il pleure dans mon coeur...")

Rain entraps me inside
the house all day long
paralyzing my soul
with the pain of its song

and turning my heart
into a dark sickroom,
watered by the rain of
endless gloom and doom.

The rain taps out a steady
code on the windowpane
without though telling me
the reason for this pain,

yet it nails me to the window
watching every raindrop land,
hoping this may be a hurt
the rain will understand.

Two-Minute Salvation

(Open Mic: To Edie Eustace who started PoetsWednesday at Barron Arts Center, the longest running poetry reading series in New Jersey.)

Although life exhales but one poetic line,
the marketplace is crowded and the stands are sagging with words
    syllables go tumbling over unrhymed syllables,
    verse climbs over verse
and you get but 2 thin minutes or less to unpack and sell your wares;

2 thin minutes to diagnose and cure the ills of the universe plus dissect
    your soul and hang it out for everyone to see the bloody mess,

2 minutes to lie on the altar where your heart is torn out and tossed
    into the shredding machine for the lack of sacrificial fire
    on the cool foreheads fencing you in

2 minutes to shove your metaphor into the mouth gaping at you
    and reach all the way down into the stomach to turn it inside out

2 minutes to strip off the clown costume and play a naked violin
    standing on the ceiling
2 minutes to get your s.o.s across an ocean of suffocating clichés
2 minutes to douse yourself with rhymes and look for matches
2 minutes to give away eternity wrapped inside a hyperbole
2 minutes to steal a pearl into the eyes before you
2 minutes on the judge's bench
2 minutes in the dock
2 minutes on the butcher block
2 minutes on the rack
2 minutes on the soapbox
2 minutes on the cross

but 2 minutes can also be the age of the universe if you have
    a well-honed secret tucked away in a pocket of your verse
and if your frantic meter doesn't cause it to sink before
    you reach a sunny shore of applause
hanging on to the 2 minutes refrain
    just 2 more minutes please
and then you can shoo me off into nevermore.

The Wild Vase

The perfect amber carnival-glass vase
must grow out of a powerfully
bulbous base and then
stretch out itself
into a slender
stem to reach
for its soul
higher up
for faith
to raise
its lips
freely
into
arcs
in a
ping
slim
long
gold
song
of high
delirium
that flares
the vase out
so wild wide
and sprays it with
untamable bouquets of
intoxicating madness-rays.
Now praise be to the master who
erects this wild vase and praise be also
to the devout lips of the wild soul who
kneeling before it lovingly prays.

The Endless End

In Memoriam Camilla

Earth to Earth

how deep below is that *earth to earth* how far down to go for *peace*
    I feel myself bend into a question mark leaning on a headstone

while our small group awkwardly gathers
    like disjointed clumps around a crumbling angel statue

while a bearded man in black talks into an old book open in his hands
    while I describe how the beloved had made fairy tales out of her nightmares
        while a middle-aged lady relates a prank they had pulled as kids

the hole stays covered up with a square piece of canvas as if for a surprise
    but then the man in black intones a few more verses and turns to me
        pointing to the canvas and the heavy earthenware container nearby

I reluctantly snatch the cover off and grab the container of ashes
    it's only then that the hole turns out to be much deeper than I'd expected

I've got to go down on my knees and finally even on elbows in the dark suit
    in order to lower the container without dropping it
        the hole keeps pulling me down not only the container

but then the container touches bottom and my hands are free of their burden
    free to prop me up and let me scramble to my feet

free of the burden but weighed down more heavily by its absence

the traffic noise downhill resumes its life but it's no longer my life that goes on
    without the life of the one the ritual is all about

while we stumble back to the cars
    the sunshine doesn't even flicker as I brush the dirt off my knees

you and I had gotten so much dirt above ground I say softly to the urn in the hole
we should be used to it

but she was so good at remembering sunshine and turned even dirt into a smile
    like I turn it into tears and stabs of memories no urn can hold

how can the sky be so bright blue on a day like this and the gravestones so gray
    if she gets one let it be hazel the color of her eyes

Eyes Closed

A house with shutters closed in broad daylight
must have a light on inside or at least a TV set,
but why you? Why don't you open your eyes?
Maybe you'd enjoy watching a daytime soap,
something more exciting than a hospital room.

I understand, believe me, I know how it goes.
Some mornings I don't feel like opening my eyes
either, preferring to untangle the problems of the night,
so take your time. But at least try to give a little wink,
a little sign that you haven't quite forgotten me...

I know you can't talk with that big tube in your mouth,
taped to your lips and wheezing like the draft in
a wind-infested attic without a message to deliver,
without a meaning to reveal that would open my eyes...
Yes, I swear I'll keep my eyes closed until you open yours!

Danse Macabre

had I only known...but I didn't, not really,
and I didn't miss the call from her...Just calling
to say hello and that I love you...and you knew
what you had to do which was not to groan...

had I only...but the countdown clock was
right in front of you and it's turned on at birth
you have to keep an eye on it
count not only the years that pass but the ones left

had I only...could you have stopped that clock
had you only had your eyes on it
rather than on the show of IV drips
the rising and falling of the chest...

had I only...it was not she who was moving
her chest but a pump...she played Coppélia
you set her clock running but forgot to tell her
about the countdown clock...just a mistake...

had I only known...but you knew what
the magician was doing was stopping the clock
and then making a robot out of her dead body
had I only...I wouldn't have watched her dance

had I only...I would've said the same when
she called me on her way to the magician's office
she called me just to say she loved me...but I
did say...didn't I...I meant to...and I did...didn't I?

*(based on a story by E.T.A. Hoffmann about a mechanical
dancing doll named Coppélia)*

My Crutch

A curtain of words,
a page torn from a dictionary;
that's what I throw on the hospital bed.

What is the opposite of orphan?

Widows and widowers go hand in hand,
but a parent, robbed of an only child, has no label,
no rubric, no box to cross off on any form,
not even on the death certificate.

What is the opposite of gray?
Black or white?

What is the opposite of melancholy?
Despair or serenity?

What is the opposite of a wreath?
A desert or a rose garden?

The roof garden of the Met Museum
or the desert around Jericho?
I'd take either if she too can come along.
What is the opposite of remembrance?
Pain or joy?

The opposite of orphan is a lonely old
geezer, sneaking into an empty cemetery
with a memory to lean on.

What's going to break first?
The question or the crutch?

The Lonely Fable

True loneliness is not hung
on a chair standing by itself
next to a plain table,
but on a table without

a single chair beside it.

Even the room where
that table is located turns
bare walls toward it.

A table by itself may not
even be a table but
a simple stand for an urn
with no words to echo,
no touches to recall.

At one time I was a table
with chairs around me,
but only one stayed for
fifty years before taken
away to be burned.

Now I am alone without
a single chair beside me,
and even I don't know
what to call myself.

The Last Xmas Tree

It was the best tree we'd ever had last Xmas,
she said when it was over, and now I'm glad
I'd let her talk me into shelling out sixty dollars
for that two-ton tree; what the hell, let her have

what she wants for Xmas! and I had the clumsy
thing put on top of the car, which was the easy part.
Carrying it into the house was the real work,
but I did it, and now I'm so glad I did, because

it turned out to be the last Xmas we were to have;
without her, how do I know which tree to pick?
Without her whimsical but dainty finger pointing to it,
no tree could ever be a proper Xmas tree.

Her Glasses

her reading glasses are a little dimmer than mine
but her TV glasses sharper and I inherited them both
now everything I read is about the myth of the cave
maybe the only book we both read and could discuss

but I don't watch family channel and she only watched
BBC news with me when she was home and there was
nothing else on and indeed she was right why bother
she lived on an island that had its own sun and rain

once there was an island we used to enjoy together
sometimes I still swim out to it unless a storm sweeps it
over me throwing it like a black hood engulfing me
because I inherited her glasses but not her eyes

The Endless End

When she turned eighteen, I set her free,
let her leave the family garden and tend to
her own flowerbed just as I stayed in
the old one minding the same old herbs.

She was more than eager to make the leap
and fence off her own flowerbed, but instead
of growing flowers she drew pictures of them,
one on top of another, with a finger in the dirt.

But stormy winds and showers washed away her
creations, erasing the flowers drawn in soil until,
after years of work, her flowerbed turned fallow
like a desert, even its outlines were hard to frame.

Now she shares a flowerbed with the whole
big family, granddad and grandmother and more,
all of them working together to grow granite slabs
that no wind can sweep away, no seasons can age.

Hope

Once a poet declared it was a mirage
toying with us earthly mortals but
admitted it was a fun game to play

without it the young would not
go ahead with the adventure of
living and making children live

without it the old would not come
to know the meaning of the troubles
they managed to endure again and again

we live through life drunk on the nectar
of hope whether it's fulfilled or not
hope is in the genes of happiness

in its delirium we plan the impossible and
struggle to succeed but we also shed the tears
of joy reminiscing about the fancy hopes of old

Like most of us, Cam remained hope forever unfulfilled,
but how painfully happy and fervent a hope it was!
It's still toying with this earthly mortal left behind.

Father's Day Parade

Okay, if I am to play the father again,
and the day's program is mine,
then let it be adventurous, I used to say,
let's go swimming in Crater Lake
if weather allows,
but if not,
let it be educational,
let's visit a historic building or a museum,
or a natural wonder,
like I planned for today;
let's visit Crystal Caves in Hellertown!
I know you've been there before
a couple of times with the group,
but you never got past the gift shop,
and now we have a chance to see
the whole place and learn all about its wonders.
Life is a learning process, as we say,
we keep accumulating loaves of wisdom
for old age,
and I'm in it now but without a crumb
for my mind to nibble on,
with you gone without a reason,
and I am still foolish enough to keep on asking why
on my first Father's Day alone;
an abandoned natural wonder,
overgrown with memories.

Funny...

how I used to bug you about your weight
and you turned yourself weightless
what's the molecular weight of the soul?
the speed of a prayer?

how I begged you to tell me what
was behind your choreographed smile
and you left stacks of diaries behind
that I'm afraid to open

how you didn't trust just one message
on the phone to get to me and
how many did you have to leave?
how many bees in the basket of a summer day?

how my cell phone rings
even if I just happen to look at it
or else it's ringing in my sinuses and
I have to accept my cell phone is dead

how I can't conjure up your face because
I don't want to see the purple and the tubes
what is the molecular weight of the soul
the ringtone of a prayer?

Maledizione! *(paraphrase on Verdi's* Rigoletto*)*

What kind of a father is he who
        lets this happen...
who, wearing the mantle of a curse,
        brings a daughter into this world?
Al mondo?
        Tutto al mondo you say?
Maledizione!
        You deserved to be deprived of her,
you wretch, you cursed creature, you...
        mia figlia per me...
indeed, how dare you say that...
        you *schiavo*...you faithful slave
of a *maledizione,*
you knew you were a curse to this world
and the world a curse to you,
        you had no right to a daughter,
you belonged in a stage lit up with daggers of jests,
        not to her world,
        not to her *tutto al mondo...*
        she's no longer *mia figlia...*
        she's no longer *per me,*
she's for another *al mondo*
        where you are not to go,
so just shut up and move on carrying
        your *maledizione* on your back
and never look back at that *tutto al mondo...*
        pray to *mia figlia* for forgiveness
drink nothing but the saliva of the curse
        on the cruel path that leads to her
it's time now for me to have a chance
        to sing to her like it has echoed
in my mind since she was born:
        Tutto al mondo è tal mia figlia per me!
And now, let the curtain drop
        Please!
But why didn't I write a happy poem on this quote
        while she was still alive? Why?
...*non morir!* now will not do...

The Weekend

The calendar now is a ghost town of empty squares,
nothing marked for this weekend;
she's not scheduled to come home.

But the measly evergreen bush I planted this spring
is greening, so she too must be doing fine.

She couldn't make it home for Xmas;
there was no point in putting up a tree, so I just got
a small potted pine for the holiday season.

Come summer, she might be home to celebrate
her Xmas present, the scrawny pine
I'd put in the ground with plenty of organic fertilizer
out front, by the road, where
sunshine lingers long enough for a prayer.

Now the little pine is greening,
so she, too, must be doing fine.

It's just that she cannot come home this weekend.
Maybe some other time;

the calendar may seem blank, but it's full of waiting
and patience like a shady graveyard where
abandoned shadows go to wait for a kinder sun.

On an Endless Road

It was my fault, same as
when going out once all dressed up
I braked too fast at the first main road
and you got some coffee spilled
on your clean shirt—See, Dad, what you did?—

Your voice was a rose petal drooping,
bright pink unable to hold on, yes,
I should've watched the traffic and my foot,
it was my fault letting you down;
your eyes turned hummingbirds standing still.

It was a holyday playing daughter and dad,
but spills and jolts too played a part.
Sorry I didn't always watch out for them
like a good dad should for a trusting child;
from now on though there'll be no more mistakes,

no more parties, no more smiles, no more spills,
no more drives, nothing to watch out for; yes,
that needle, too, in the allergy office was my fault,
and now no more—See Dad what you did?—
no more stop signs—

       we're on an endless road.

The Lost Raindrop

it's as if raindrops were popping up
from the grass, from asphalt and umbrellas,
headed straight up into the dripless blue
to smudge it up with their dank touches
and leave it looking used,
in need of a paint job or a bulldozer...

it's as if I was trying to attach
a golden leaf back to a maple branch
instead of treasuring the gold as it is...

I keep trying to force mementoes back to life

catch the ball of time and toss it back to her

I'll have to stop trying to go backwards
before I find myself nowhere

a raindrop suspended in motionless mist

and I will not find the one I lost
by going back
there's no back there, there

Acknowledgments

The poems in this book first appeared or are scheduled to appear in the following publications:

Arch & Quiver: Wozzeck Paraphrases

Ashvamegh: Poetry Paraphrase

Aurorean: Redemption Circa 20th Century C.E., Trail to Timelessness

Big Hammer: Committing Poetry in Public, The Ratgod, The Sweet Stink of Money, On Exhibit

Black Mountain Press: Her Glasses, Hope

Blueline Review: Stealing Mountains

California Quarterly: Springing, Canyon Dreams

Caveat Lector: Midden of Dreams:

Ceremony: Art-Drunk Midnight

Chiron: Friday in MOMA with George, Tightrope Too

Clare: The War's Unfinished Nocturne

Colere: The Eighth Dwarf

Consequences: War & Peace in Budapest

Cotyleon: Up and/or Down

Delaware Valley Poets: Redwood Chair at Rest

Deronda: In No Man's Land, Silence versus Noise, The Country of the Soul

Deus Loci: The City on the Hill

Diner: Rat Factory

Dream Network: Inside, Outside in the Jungle

Drexel: Dark Windows in the Fog

Eclipse: Two-Sided Mistake

Exit 13: Saturday Morning in Warren, Mount Minsi, Brooklyn Bat

Flaming Arrow (Ireland): Anyway, The Doves

Gargoyle: War Bread

Grain (Canada): Morning Metamorphosis

Green Hill Literary Lantern: A Night Outside My Head

Harp Strings: The Wild Vase

Home Planet News: Ex Libris, Short Course on Freedom

Ibbetson Review: The Orphan Key

Iconoclast: Winter Dead

Illuminations: The Last Wind and the Last Man on Earth

Libido: The Fourth Position

Into the Teeth of the Wind: Night Walk

Iodine: Street Ballad, Sudden and Reckless Peace

Iota: Pedestal City Revisited

Invisible Shadows: In Sun's Shadow

Lake Tahoe Writers: From a Hiker's Diary

Lincoln Poets Literary Journal: Free Ride

Linkways (UK): Brief Belief

Literature Today: Father's Day Parade

Lit Magazine: Tales from the Trap, Drunken Deer Eyes

Love After Seventy Anthology: Passing the Seventy-Mile Mark, The Second Coming of Antichrist

Magma (UK): Armistice Day Parade

Main Channel Voices: County Road

Midwest Review: Discovery of the Sky

Muse: Summer's Throat

Nanny Fanny: Twists and Turns of Map Noir

Nebo: Two-Minute Salvation

Neovictorian/Deronda: The Fat Lady Sings, Bombs in Armchairs

Of/With: Years Stalking

Orbis: The Fences I've Climbed Over

Out of Line: Dona Mihi Pacem

Ozone Park: Last Look at JFK Below

Patterson Literary Review: The Endless End

Pedestal: War in Snow

Pegasus: Desert Stone

Peer Poetry Review (UK): Insomniac Dreams

Pirene: Chamber Opera in Ten Acts

Poem: A Night at the Opera

Poesy: Rumors of the Night

Poetry Pacific: Geometric Mythology

Poetry Salzburg Review (Austria): Macedonian Dreams, Costume Drama
 in the Nude

Ragazine: Feelings, Earth to Earth, The Last Xmas Tree, Maledizione!

Ravensperch: The Hero of My Childhood, Laconic Bulls

Rambunctious Review: Violent Concerto No. 1

Red Wheelbarrow: The Taste of Blood

Rhino: The History of Nothing

Rive Gauche: The Midnight Trolley

Riversong: Birds of Different Feather

Roux: Sunset Dives into Lake Balaton

Rubies In The Dark (UK): Echoes of a Golden Age, The Grand Bazaar,
 A Variation on a Theme by Verlaine

Salit: Immortality Denied

Same: The 1st Day of a Long Winter

Samizdada: Monosyllabic Words

Sanskrit: Erecting New Ruins Every Day

Shades of December: Postcard from Budapest

Slant: Snow-Sun of a Nor'easter

Small Pond: The Silent Dreamer

Speedpoets (Australia): Chase of the Night

Stillwater Review: Song of a Green-Glazed Tile, An Idol Not Cruel

South Dakota Review: Hiking the Canada Dry Trail

Taproot: What Finality Feels Like

Tipton Journal: The Trees of Eden

Twilight Endings: Still Life in a Shattered Mirror

Untamed Ink: Hubcap Let Loose

US1 Worksheets: Frying Pan Morning

Valley Voices: Belgian Still Life Without Canvas, Squirrel Gods

Verdad: Summer Evening Sonatina

Visions International: Trans Gypsy Moth

Water Wood: Armageddon Again

Wordwrights: Rue du Revenant

Writers Journal: The Implanted Epitaph

About the Author

PAUL SOHAR washed up on these shores as a student refugee in the aftermath of the 1956 uprising in his homeland, Hungary. He ended his higher education with a BA in philosophy and took a day job in a research lab while writing in every genre, publishing seventeen volumes of translations from Hungarian, the latest being *The Conscience of Trees* (Ragged Sky Press, 2018). His own poetry: *Homing Poems* (Iniquity Press, 2006) and *The Wayward Orchard* (Wordrunner Press Prize winner, 2011). Prose works: "True Tales of a Fictitious Spy" (Synergebooks, 2006) and a collection of one-act plays from One Act Depot (Saskatoon, Canada, 2014). Magazines: *Agni, Gargoyle, Kenyon Review, Rattle, Trajectory,* and numerous others.

Paul Sohar with his daughter, Camilla

CPSIA information can be obtained
at www.ICGtesting.com
Printed in the USA
FSHW012113090120
65737FS